People vote for the **president** and other leaders.

Not everyone can vote.

People vote for the president every four years.

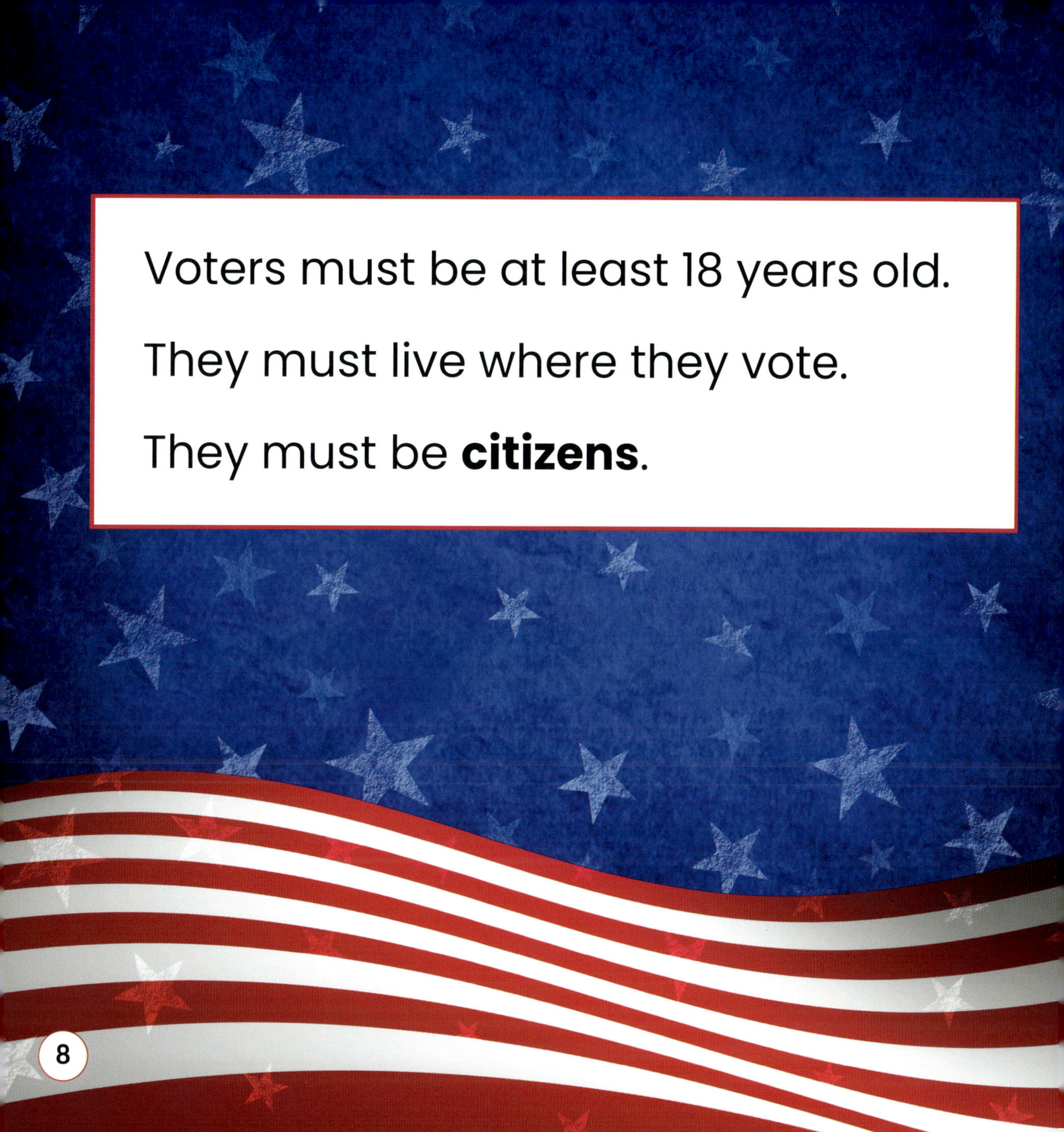

Voters must be at least 18 years old.

They must live where they vote.

They must be **citizens**.

VOTE

Voters learn about those who want to be leaders.

They think about who to choose.

Voters want good leaders.

POLITICS
BREAKING NEWS

Election Day is the special day for voting.

The **ballot** has the names of those who want to be leaders.

Voters mark the person they want.

Each person may mark only one ballot.

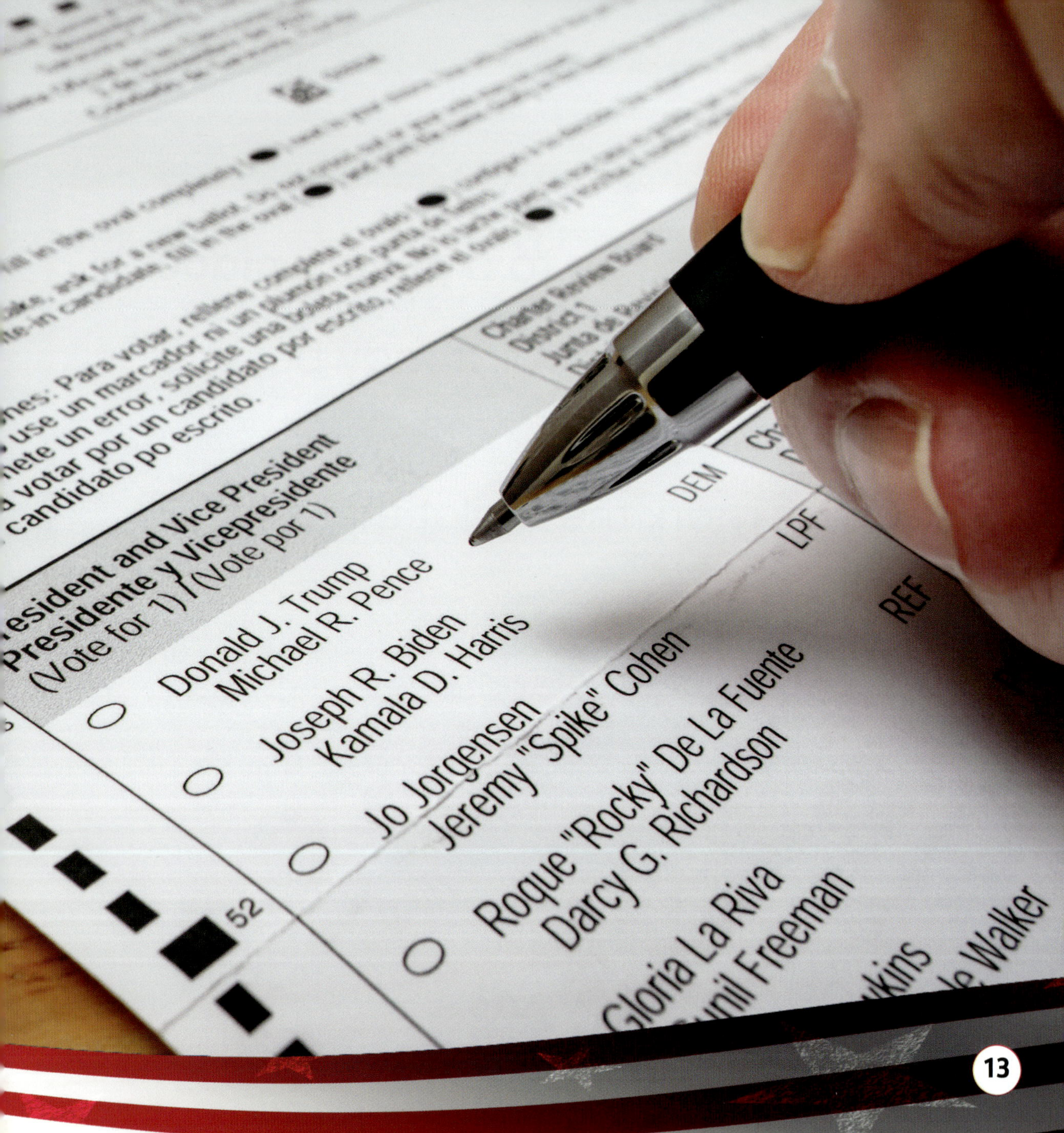
resident and Vice President
Presidente y Vicepresidente
(Vote for 1) / (Vote por 1)
Donald J. Trump
Michael R. Pence
Joseph R. Biden
Kamala D. Harris
DEM
Jo Jorgensen
Jeremy "Spike" Cohen
LPF
Roque "Rocky" De La Fuente
Darcy G. Richardson
REF
Gloria La Riva
52

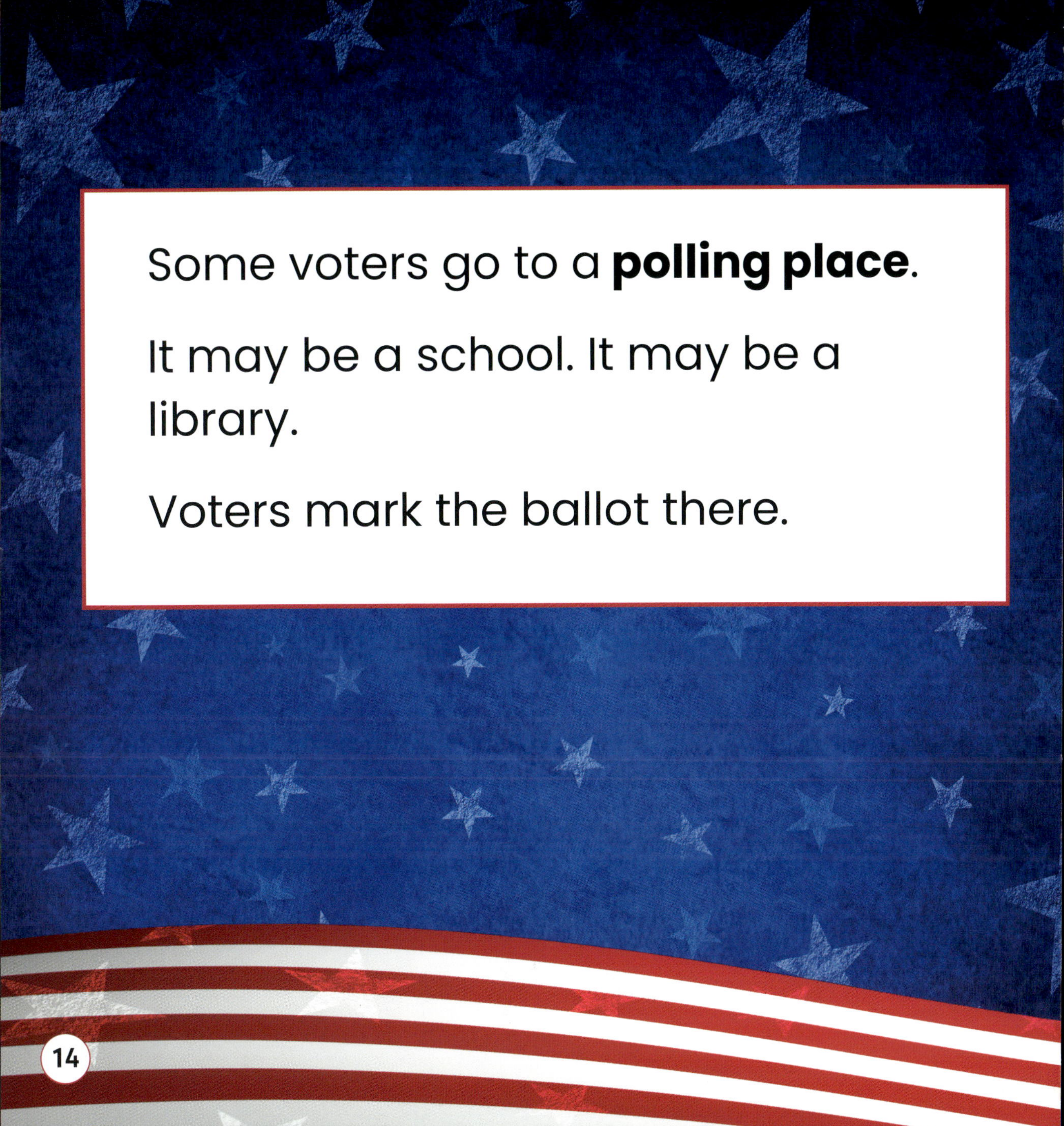

Some voters go to a **polling place**.

It may be a school. It may be a library.

Voters mark the ballot there.

VOTE
HERE

Other voters stay home.

Their ballot comes in the mail.

The voter marks it and sends it back.

Elections Official
123 Campaign Street
Township, State 45678
VOTE-BY-MAIL
BUSINESS

All votes are counted.

The person with the most votes wins.

Breaking News

'he Latest...

Results

'he Results Are In!

Result Tally

est Results

Results

Final Outcom

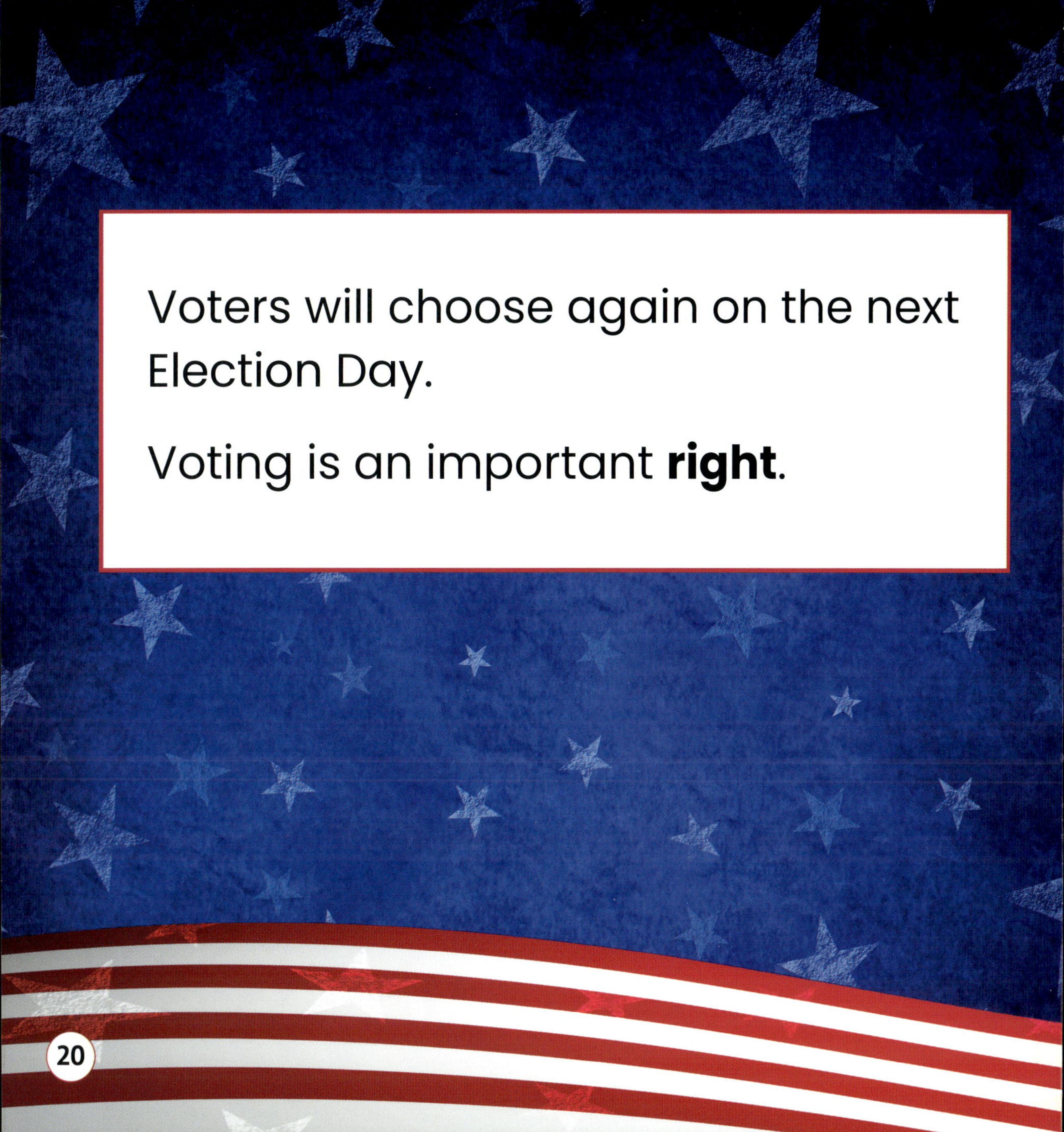

Voters will choose again on the next Election Day.

Voting is an important **right**.

YOUR
✓OTE
MATTERS

Words to Know

ballot (BA-luht): a form where people mark their vote

choice (choys): the act of picking one out of a group

citizens (SIH-tuh-zens): people who are members of a country and have the rights of that country

polling place (POH-ling playc): the building where people go to vote

president (PREZ-uh-dent): the head of the government in some countries, such as the United States

right (rite): something a person is allowed to do under the law

vote (voht): to make a choice for or against someone or something

Index

Comprehension Questions

1. When do people vote for leaders?
   a. on St. Patrick's Day
   b. on Thanksgiving Day
   c. on Election Day

2. Everyone must make their voting choice on a ________.
   a. website
   b. cellphone
   c. ballot

3. A polling place can be
   a. a library.
   b. a school.
   c. both A and B.

4. **True or False:** Voting can be done through the mail.

5. **True or False:** Voters must be at least 21 years old.

Answers
1. c 2. c 3. c 4. True 5. False

About the Author

Tracy Vonder Brink enjoys learning about the United States. She votes every Election Day. She lives in Cincinnati with her husband, two daughters, and two rescue dogs.

Written by: Tracy Vonder Brink
Design by: Kathy Walsh
Editor: Kim Thompson

Photographs/Shutterstock: Cover © Orlowski Designs LLC, ©Lightspring, ©Vertes Edmond Mihai: Pg 4-21 ©Lightspring: Pg 3 ©Monkey Business Images: Pg 5 ©Alexandru Nika: Pg 7 ©Minerva Studio: Pg 9 ©vesperstock: Pg 11 © Monkey Business Images: Pg 13 ©The Toidi: Pg 15 ©Andrey_Popov: Pg 17 ©Castleski: Pg 19 ©iQoncept: Pg 21 ©StunningArt

Library of Congress PCN Data
The Right to Vote / Tracy Vonder Brink
Civic Readiness
ISBN 978-1-63897-086-6 (hard cover)
ISBN 978-1-63897-172-6 (paperback)
ISBN 978-1-63897-258-7 (EPUB)
ISBN 978-1-63897-344-7 (eBook)
Library of Congress Control Number: 2021945262

Printed in the United States of America.

Seahorse Publishing Company
www.seahorsepub.com

Copyright © 2022 **SEAHORSE PUBLISHING COMPANY**

All rights reserved. No part of this publication may be reproduced, stored in a retrieval system or be transmitted in any form or by any means, electronic, mechanical, photocopying, recording, or otherwise, without the prior written permission of Seahorse Publishing Company.

Published in the United States
Seahorse Publishing
PO Box 771325
Coral Springs, FL 33077

This is an **elephant**.

Words to Know

ears

elephant

gray

herds

trunk

tusks

Alicia Rodriguez

TABLE OF CONTENTS

A Pelican Book